T0106456

Making Conversation Work for You

Dr. Paul R. Friesen

iUniverse, Inc.
New York Bloomington

Making Conversation Work for You

iUniverse books may be ordered through booksellers or by contacting:

iUniverse
1663 Liberty Drive
Bloomington, IN 47403
www.iuniverse.com
1-800-Authors (1-800-288-4677)

ISBN: 978-1-4502-2409-3 (pbk)
ISBN: 978-1-4502-2410-9 (ebook)

Printed in the United States of America

iUniverse rev. date: 4/5/10

Making Conversation

Work for YOU

Includes

Conversation, Drama, Grammar, Games

FUN

Dr. Paul R. Friesen

Making Conversation Work for You

Key words --- communication, drama, conversation, vocabulary, ESL, fun

Author Dr. Paul R. Friesen

Table of Contents

Dedication

Over many years this idea has stewed in my head. I have tried different ideas and have had input from many people stirring me on. I would like to dedicate this project to my grandfather, now deceased. He had the **DNA** that never was satisfied with the status quo. He went to places where others would not go. He was criticized for his views and never had a chance to put them out in a medium.

I would like to give special thanks to **Sidney**, a former co-worker and teacher, who has encouraged me through the process of making this idea come to this format. Without her I would have wandered a bit more and I appreciate her input.

I would like to give kudos to **Dr. Roy Hewitt Beadle Jr,** , who has pushed me on to finish the project. His vision and the contacts he has made, has pushed this into the public view faster and with more integrity than I could have ever dreamed.

There are others who have visited my home page and given me encouragement in many other projects as well. There are just too many to name. There will also be those who want to interact to make it better. These are also encouragers and needed for anything to keep up to date as culture and education moves forward. A big thank you for the future.

Dr. Paul R. Friesen

Making TESOL more effective in a mono-cultural setting.

Basic Premise –

TESOL is the basic educational pedagogy for teaching English as Second Language acquisition. The pedagogy is reasonable but the normal application has some flaws. The flaw as I see it is that most books and applications are for intake into an English speaking culture. Using the same pedagogy in a mono-non-English culture needs to be adjusted to allow for the focus on the elements of culture rather than precise cultural perspectives. This is because there are no precise across-the-board equal proportioned idioms and colloquialisms or word usages. Each word can be twisted and turned depending on the geographical area the speaker lives in. The same goes for pronunciation.

The Elements –

Therefore the elements that should be focused on are Time, Action, Moving, Emotion, and Equality. Under Emotion the designation of percentages reflects the use of emotion, body language and language. The percentage as taught by this author is 50 - 25 - 25.

The Method --

The method of teaching is a reflection of grammar as it reflects the TAME method with an over arching rule of Equal. Teaching these elements as basic rules for listening comprehension, writing, and speaking can result in a stronger communication ideal. Teaching the elements of tame will make the cultural nuances and usage's easier to gain a basic understanding of, and easier to respond to.

A Closer look --

Looking at the Basic English conversation taught leaves the word uses very narrow. Understanding the idea of the time element allows us to use different words to denote not only time but a combination of time action and emotion. For example, "Yesterday I went shopping". This is a basic sentence giving time and action. Now let's add emotion, "Yesterday was fun. I went shopping." "Was fun", are not hard words but it does make the two sentences more emotive, more realistic, and less hard and stilted. This in turn translates into better body language, down to good simple grammar, and overall better communication, which is the key of TESOL.

Problem Possibilities -

As a Native speaker it is hard to think and teach the passive voice. It is not as natural as the active voice. It takes great effort to do this. This difficulty is not insurmountable. Rather with a little reflection about the essence of normal conversation we will find we use it quite often. To teach it makes us break with the norms and change the beginning questions in our conversation.

Moving away from grammar oriented conversation books. To combine grammar and conversation is usually what is done. The question is whether it is how we want to teach it. In a standard University class or book there is a new grammar lesson with each week. This means that the student must absorb the grammar and lose focus on the conversation. This defeats the purpose of teaching conversation. Moving away from these books allows a refocus on the communication aspect of conversation teaching.

Problem Solutions -

Solutions are varied and many but the question remains how effective they are. In South Korea it is assumed that there has been a foundation of learning that has been laid. The solution is then to build on the foundation. The foundation that should be laid after several years of English classes both public and private is poorly made. Therefore it is imperative to rebuild the foundation so that the creative structure and beauty can be achieved. To do this I would propose that the structure of conversation be the beginning of this change. Once the structure of basic "question and answer", "listen and repeat key words", is understood, understanding and building vocabulary can be achieved more effectively. Too many students learn the idioms and phrases which are not in their nature, which in turn makes them awkward in presentation.

The Nature of Conversation Learning -

In the blank slate theory it is easy to make new roads and impressions. When there is already pattern made change can be made but with some difficulty. Assuming that the students in TESOL have an already printed pattern the nature of learning conversation must be linked to these patterns. To do this the teacher must understand the nature of the conversation and how it relates to the learners previous imprints of conversation. In English, as in all languages, there are many ways to communicate. Conversation is just one method.

Conversation is dissimilar to writing, but if the foundation of writing has been established conversation becomes easier. Movie English can be a good way to learn conversation. At the same time it can be the weakest link to learning conversation. Yet, it is one of the most popular ways to try. Most of the conversations in movies are lost in the speed of the movie and the noise of the background. Sitcoms are better but the nuances are usually not understood. Therefore, the conversation links and framework are left in the dust. It does not reflect a real life scenario. Drama is great fun but again the conversation learning factor is limited because of the stress on body language etc.

Understanding the nature of conversation as it relates to the imprint can accelerate the understanding of communication in general. Conversation, in real life, is just communication of information. Therefore we should not focus so much on the grammar and the development of a semi-spontaneous response to what has been heard. Learning to recognize the key elements of a conversation gives direction to and embellishment of the information wanted.

Focusing on grammar, as found in books like the _Interchange_ Series, are not proven to be effective. Grammar takes more time and is more relevant to writing not conversation. Therefore we need to change our focus into a more strategic building of conversation understanding.

Conversation building is about attitudes and understanding the nature of what information you want to acquire. It is imperative to use a variety of the same idea because it is the nature of conversation. There is no one perfect way to say things. To memorize perfectly means that you have already lost the nature of conversation per se. Conversation is about key words, or the bricks, and the mortar which are the words that seem insignificant but hold it together.

In a mono versus multi – cultural setting the ideas like immersion are very different. In the same breath having groups of the same language group huddled together after a class is also defeating the purpose. There needs to be more of a "go out and do it on your own" idea. Putting students in situation where they need to communicate. Left alone in the dark to find the door, so to speak. Grammar is then given a rough ride as real words necessary to communicate come forward. It is at this point that the understanding of the mortar words or the need to learn them first, becomes important.

Synchronicity -

If you teach in South Korea you will find a large gap in the teaching and the students. It is understood that the students will all learn differently, that is a given. On the other hand there is no learning synchronization. Without a systematic synchronization of learning there become just pieces which are disconnected. Therefore the overlaps and the gaps become disjointed and almost dysfunctional. The goal of the teacher is to bring these pieces into linked rationality. The students in a mono-cultural setting do not interact much with other cultures. The farther you get out of the large metropolitan hubs the more true this becomes. Therefore the need for synchronicity is even more urgent.

Building better Foundations -

If we accept the fact that there is a lack of synchronicity but not a lack of knowledge, we need to tap into the areas where the learning has resided. We need to analyze what has been imprinted and what is necessary for better communication. This can be done by listening to the student. In a monoculture a teacher will find the students have similar problems associated with transliteration.

In multi-cultural material the assumption is that there are various problems. In a mono-cultural setting the needs are similar so the solutions can be generalized. The weaknesses are equally similar and leveling is easier.

Building foundations is easy if you take apart conversation pieces. What is important and what is not? For example, in Hangul the numbers are important but they are opposite to American English. Foreigners make jokes and shake their head but this does not mean that there needs to be a conversation structure change. Rather, the need to change the strategy of teaching should be changed because it is a mono-culture. By designing books that reflect this will stimulate or accelerate the student's acquirement of the target language.

A good everyday example of this fact is the advertising you find in South Korea. It is opposite to Western thinking, higher to lower versus lower to higher. Should we make Korea change her way of marketing or should we challenge ourselves to develop a strategy to communicate better. In reality the market is not the foreigner but the Korean. Therefore the Korean structure of thinking should be assimilated into the marketing strategy. What is important comes last not first. It makes sense in a mono-cultural world to bring the foundation of learning as close as possible to the market you want to reach.

Therefore we must use the structure already imprinted and build from it. We do not need to break it down and rebuild it. In this paper I will use **T.A.M.E.** as the acronym for this new strategy. This will also determine the strategy to use in putting all the abstract pieces of learning into a logical interface for communication.

T is for time. Time is an important part of communication and conversation. We do not always say it but we need to understand how important it is.

A is for action. To communicate action will determine the reaction we receive when we speak. Is it an emergency or not? Is what we want to communicate important or not? By understanding the nature of how we communicate action we determine the response we want.

M is for motion/moving. In grammar you would use the "ing" most of the time, but not always. Understanding the nature of moving adds a component to the action word. There are elements of speed and space moved. An added dimension to the basic idea, but which determine your communication of the action you want.

E is for emotion. This is the last letter but the most important element of communicating in our conversation. It is here that the hardest problem is. In the mono-culture of South Korea emotion in communication is often harsh and limited. People yell instead of using their body to communicate. Emotion is, in my opinion, the key to communication. To use words which express the emotion you want, in combination with body language, will do more than enhance the conversation, it will appreciate the value of your communication. This will make it more effective and enjoyable and begin linking the past learning into a synchronized structure. This in turn will stimulate the desire for interaction with other cultures.

In a sentence, it will T.A.M.E. the fear brought on by dysfunctional unsynchronized learning.

In Conclusion

Using a sentence structure closer to the student's primary thinking processes and language, combined with assigning values to words previously learned will:

1. Link together the previous learned ideas into synchronization.
2. Through synchronization, **strengthen** the foundational skills for conversation.
3. Give **confidence** to the student to reach out and communicate with other cultures.

100
Words

A revaluation of previously learned vocabulary

Activity

The idea behind the 100 words is to

1) Know how many words or depth of vocabulary a student has.
2) Use the words to give emotional values to the words from a base.

This will help the student think about each word differently. It is not just a word but a value to a conversation and communicates values to the rest of the words. Developing vocabulary in this way, allows the links to the base emotion to give better understanding of other words that are not in the listeners vocabulary at the time they are spoken.

By developing quick links to base emotion words allows for faster vocabulary building and better verbalization of emotion in conversation. Therefore the last 100 Words page challenges the student to think about the emotional values of word they use. After this is worked through, the continued emphasis on these four areas, which are critical to good communication, will strengthen and build better communication techniques and strategies.

Emotion accounts for a large part of communication. Therefore the need to understand the emotional values of words is vital for communication in ANY language.

These words will be referred to in different sections of the book. There is also a second 100 words section. Using values of words versus the base interpretation will help the student understand how to use a dictionary as well.

The problem with many dictionaries is that there are just base structure values and not meaning values. The student chooses different words based on structure. This confuses the student when they are constantly rebuffed or corrected by others. Revaluing the vocabulary for good communication will help retention, comprehension, and usage of words otherwise hid.

This book is not a vocabulary builder. Rather, it utilizes what is already known and gives a framework to restructure these words. The student can then use the base idea of revaluation to build their vocabulary in areas where they need to.

Time

1._hour_   2._____   3._____   4._____   5._____

6._____   7.___day___   8._____   9._____   10._____

11._____   12._____   13._____   14._____   15._____

16._____   17._____   18._____   19._____   20._____

21._____   22._____   23._____   24._____   25._____

Action

26._____   27._____   28.__watch_   29._____   30._____

31._____   32._____   33._____   34._____   35.___play__

36._____   37._____   38._____   39._____   40._____

41._____   42._____   43._____   44._____   45._____

46._____   47._____   48._____   49._____   50._____

෧ ෧ ෧ Notes ෧ ෧ ෧

Low – Time words can be simple and basic like: hour, minute, Monday, Tuesday, January, March, etc.

Intermediate – Look for more complex ideas like: often, sometimes, soon, etc. In Action look for words that describe speed or the nature of an action.

High – Look for a phrase or preposition that denotes time like: on the weekend, before …, and after. Action words should also reflect this level like: place on…, take it …, to the, etc.

Motion

51._____   52._____   53._____   54._shopping   55._____

56._____   57._____   58._studying   59._____   60._____

61._____   62._____   63._____   64._____   65._____

66._____   67._____   68._____   69._____   70._____

71._____   72._____   73._____   74._____   75._____

Emotion

76._____   77._____   78._____   79._____   80._____

81.___sad___   82._____   83._____   84._____   85._____

86._____   87._____   88._____   89._miffed__   90._____

91._____   92._____   93._____   94._____   95.__blue___

96._____   97._____   98._____   99._____   100._____

ଔ ଔ ଔ Notes ଔ ଔ ଔ

Low – Motion words can use the "ing" ending at this level. Emotion words should reflect basic emotions like: sad, angry, etc.

Intermediate – Look for more complex ideas like: forward, side to side, etc. Emotion words should move away from basic like: angry ~ upset, depressed ~blue, envy, etc. Using endings like hope**ful**, bad**ly**, etc should be encouraged.

High – Look for a phrase or preposition that denotes time like: going crazy, or zany, eccentric, etc. Words that give motion and emotion like ~ to and from ~ denote motion and imply movement in a direction. Emotion words fine tune the larger simpler words like angry and sad. A good exercise here is to use a thesaurus to find words that can be used as replacement words but have a different level of emotional implication.

Writing

Step 1
    Choose one (1)
        TIME/action/motion/emotion
                    word from the list.
    Write them in the boxes.

EXAMPLE

❶ Hour/play/hitting/hard	❷
❸	❹

15

Step 2

Make a sentence with each of the four words. Write them in the boxes below.

You can mix the order of the words to help you.

EXAMPLE

❶ At five o'clock I play baseball, hitting the ball hard.

❷

❸

❹

Step 3   Read them **out loud** in front of the class.

Describe
Yourself

A focus on Is and Has
in the Time element
of
Conversation

Grammar Rule

IS

In Grammar there is a rule that can help you think, write, and be better understood. The **RULE is that EVERYTHING in an English sentence _NEEDS TO BE EQUAL_**. This means that A = B

        (EXAMPLE —   I AM A BOY.   I = BOY;   HE IS A BOY— HE = BOY.)

IS = time communication

IS + ING = NOW +.

    If you use _IS + ING_ you tell the other person the _TIME_ of the action.

Example — I am having a good time.

    I = _now_ and _continuing_ to have a good time.

    He is playing on the computer.

    He = _now_ and _continuing_ to play on the computer.

Note: When you use "is" or "is + ing" you communicate equal

                        or a _TIME_ of action.

Has

Has is a word that tells a person that needs a person place or thing (noun). It tells the listener that you possess the person, place, or thing. So these two ideas need to be learned in   combination. These two words or ideas go together ALL the time.

Example — He _has_ a nice car = He owns or drives a nice car.

    His car is nice. =   He owns or drives a nice car.

    He **has** a nice watch. = You like his watch

    His watch is nice.   =   You like his watch.

Note — Use He / She / It _WITH HAS_ and

               His / Her / Its with _THE OBJECT_

Writing

1. | Look at your partner and write five (5) sentences using **HAS** |

1. _____

2. _____

3. _____

4. _____

5. _____

| **D** |

The letter **D** tells me the **TIME** of the action.

The letter D tells me the time of the action. This is harder because English action words do not always use the D but change their spelling. As a rule it is the D that determines the communication of time.

Example — He play**ed** a computer game.   **(He + D)**

Problem —

> The problem here is there is **no time word** to help me understand **WHEN** he played his computer game.

Correction

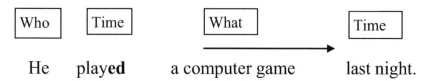

Who	Time	What	Time
He	play**ed**	a computer game	last night.

Note: The "D" = *PAST TIME AND "LAST NIGHT" = THE SAME TIME.*
NOW COMMUNICATION IS UNDERSTOOD.

Writing

Look at your 100 Words and choose **TIME** and **ACTION** words to make 5 sentences with **D** or **PAST TENSE**.

Example: day (time)   watch (action)

One day I watched the birds at the park.

1. _____

2. _____

3. _____

4. _____

5. _____

ଓଃ ଓଃ ଓଃ Notes ଓଃ ଓଃ ଓଃ

Low – For low learners concentrate on the simplicity of time and action need to be communicated in the same time frame.

Intermediate – For intermediate level learners focus on the assumed time frame. This can be seen in the example. "One day" can be any day. The action "watched" is in the past tense. The ASSUMPTION is that "one day" is ASLO past.

Advanced – For advanced learners the structure may be more complex and the student should use prepositions and other connection words.

S

~   The letter **S** is often used to tell me <u>**WHO**</u> is speaking.

~~   *S* at the end of a word communicates *WHO* and *WHEN* or *HOW MANY.*

~~~   The letter *S* is often missed in Korean English learning but it is an important communication letter. It is also a useful letter to learn to finish words.

He/She/It **+ *S*** help me understand *WHO* you are talking about.

He/She/It **+ *S*** help me understand *WHAT* you are talking about.

Example — He play**s** the computer game. (He **+ *S***)

Problem —
    The problem here is there is **no word** to help me understand **WHERE** he plays his computer game. If you add the **WHERE** you will not have so many questions and frustrations.

CORRECTION —

WHO	WHAT	WHERE	WHEN

He **plays**   a computer game   in his bedroom   at night.

ℭℜ ℭℜ ℭℜ   Notes   ℭℜ ℭℜ ℭℜ

Using *S* tells us two things.

FIRST it can tell us *WHO* is doing the action.
          In this correction He plays **tells you this.**
SECOND, it tells us that *PLAY* is a verb not a noun.
          He is doing the action PLAY.

*Have the student fill in a **TIME** word or phrase to help this sentence communicate better.*

Look at your 100 Words and choose TIME and ACTION words to make 8 sentences with **S** or present tense.

Example – hour (time)   watch   (action)

He watches his children for hours.

1._____

2._____

3._____

4._____

5,_____

6._____

7_____

8._____

෬ ෬ ෬ Notes ෬ ෬ ෬

— THE ACTION IS **BEFORE** THE TIME.
THE ACTION **FOLLOWS** THE PERSON.

SPECIAL NOTE
IF YOU change this order *YOU WILL GO TO THE PAST TENSE.*

---- For hours *HE WATCHED* his children.

Putting It all together

STEP 1

Collect all your sentences in the grammar sections and describe your partner.

Example —

He **has** a nice watch.
He play**ed** a computer game last night.
He play**s** a computer game in his bedroom.

STEP 2

Put them in a paragraph so you can **read them** in front of a class.

My partner has a nice watch. He plays computer games in his bedroom at night. He played a computer game last night.

You have made 18 sentences. **PUT THEM ALL INTO A PARAGRAPH TO DESCRIBE THE PERSON SITTING BESIDE YOU.**

My partner **has** a nice watch. He **plays** computer games in his bedroom at night. He **played** a computer game last night.

_____

_____

_____

_____

_____

_____

_____

STEP 3   The Dialogue

Use your sentences to create a dialogue. A dialogue is basically
QUESTION — ANSWER — QUESTION — ANSWER
Add an expression and you can have fun. Let's do it.
USE BODY LANGUAGE like waving your hands, etc.

Intro/ Q	Jake: Hey Sue! Did you see the new Professor yet?
Answer / Q	Sue: No I haven't. What is he wearing?
Answer /	Jake: Well, **he has** a nice watch. He **is** also **wearing** a green suit jacket. He **has** blue hair and he **is wearing** a purple tie.
Q/ Answer	Sue: Really? I have been in the Library all morning. Maybe George has seen him. Hey George! Have you seen the new Professor?
ANSWER/ Q	George: Yes. I think so. What **is** he **wearing**?
ANSWER/ Q	Sue: Hmm. I think **he is wearing** a pink shirt and orange pants. Have you seen him?
ANSWER/ QUESTION	George: No I haven't, but maybe Henry has. Hey Henry! Have you seen the new Professor?

෬ ෬ ෬ Notes ෬ ෬ ෬

-- The question and answer are not always from the same person. The sequence is the same, and makes for a good conversation.

--- Sue says, "Really?" and answers her own question and then asks a question.

---- **CHANGE THE IDEAS** like "Library" or color.
Have students **ACT THIS OUT** and ask another student the question, "Have you seen the new professor?"

| STEP 4 | Keep Going |

Henry: _____

_____:

_____

_____:

_____:

_____:

_____:

_____:

_____:

_____:

ADD MORE TO INCLUDE ALL STUDENTS IN THE CLASS.

Good questions to understand the nature of Conversation

"Hello" is the most common, or "Hi". Each situation needs more thought. So if you use "hello", use more words to *INVITE* the person to communicate with you.

Using TIME—ACTION– MOTION—EMOTION words will help.

Practice your invitations to communicate the emotion that is equal (=) to how you want them to respond.

Example --

1. An invitation to a party. You must invite a new person to it.

   ME: HI JOAN. MY FRIENDS ARE HAVING A PARTY WOULD YOU LIKE TO COME TO IT?

Answer I want is..........?

Enthusiastic — **JOAN: YES, I WOULD LOVE TO COME. WHERE IS IT?**

Polite refusal — No. Thanks. I have other appointments. Maybe another time.

෬ ෬ ෬ **Notes** ෬ ෬ ෬

Notice that the invitation does not have any emotion words.

THE RESPONSE HAS THE EMOTION WORDS.

**** By using "would", a polite word, you are suggesting an emotional answer.

In the following situations have the students write
one enthusiastic and one polite refusal.

For _HOMEWORK_ have them write real life situations to practice in class.

2. You are wanting to find a date.

      The aAnswer I want ---   _____

Enthusiastic   _____

Polite refusal _____

3. You want to return a pair of pants but you need to find the right person.

      Answer I want ----

Enthusiastic   _____

Polite refusal _____

4. You want to talk to your boss about something personal.

      Answer I want ----

Enthusiastic   _____

Polite refusal _____

5. You want to apologise to someone but they are busy.

      Answer I want ----

Enthusiastic   _____

Polite refusal _____

6. You are traveling on the subway and you need to get out, but there are too many people.

      Answer I want ----

Enthusiastic   _____

Polite refusal _____

7. Homework — You must write 2 situations when

YOU NEEDED TO MAKE AN INTRODUCTION **+**
which words you used.

Circle (enthusiastic) / polite refusal

Situation -- _____

_____

Answer I wanted ---

_____

_____

Answer I received --- enthusiastic / polite refusal

_____

_____

Situation -- _____

_____

Answer I wanted ---

_____

_____

Answer I received --- enthusiastic / polite refusal

_____

_____

What do I want to know?
What information do I want to ask about?

This is important when you enter a conversation. If you do not know what you want it is hard to ask good questions.

Good questions get good answers.

Sample Conversation —

Jake — Hello!
Sue — Hello! How are you?
Jake — I am fine thank you, and you?
Sue — Me too, and you?
Jake — Me too.

What information did you get from this person?

A. lots of information
B. a little information
C. feeling information
D. no information

What do I want _you_ to hear?

I wanted to hear some information about YOU.

❧ ❧ ❧ Notes ❧ ❧ ❧

Introductions give the direction or topic you want to talk about. If you have no plan you will end the conversation quickly like the sample above.

PRACTICE THESE QUESTIONS AND GET THE INFORMATION **YOU** WANT TO HEAR?

Introduction

Jake — Hello!

Better   Sue — Hello! How are you **feeling** today?

BEST   **SUE — HELLO! HOW IS YOUR DAY GOING?**

Answer

Better   Jake — I 'm feeling (tired, angry, great, upset,…), and you?

BEST   **JAKE – MY DAY IS GOING NOT TOO BAD, BUT THERE HAVE BEEN SOME STRESS POINTS, AND YOURS?**

What do I want to know?
What information do I want to ask about?

Sue — Well, _____

Are you feeling the same?

Jake -- _____

Sue -- _____

Jake -- _____

Sue -- _____

Jake -- _____

ଔ ଔ ଔ   **Notes**   ଔ ଔ ଔ

Continue this conversation asking GOOD QUESTIONS so that you can get better answers. Choose a topic to talk about if the students have trouble continuing the conversation. Give each group of two a different topic so that there are a wide variety of ideas to practice. Have the students read each with emotion in their voice. The emotion should reflect their response. Practice the positive and the negative.

Everything must be equal

This means that what you say must be equal.
Time words must = action words must = person words.

Example --

Problem sentence

She　　　　is sit　　　under a table.
Subject　　　verb　　　　object.

Explanation --　　　　　　　**Correction**

S = time (present) because of she　　　She sit**s** **under a table.**

"**S**" equals **a one time** action. One action. The time is *now*.

ing = time (continuing action)　　　She + is sitt**ing under a table.**

"is + ing" equals the action that starts and continues.

NOTE — THERE ARE TWO PROBLEMS IN THIS SENTENCE.
　　　1. **The verb tense is not = with the subject SHE.**
　　　2. There is a *start action* but *no finish*.

How long is she under the table?
Will she stay under the table?

The TIME *MUST* = *THE ACTION*
you want to **communicate**.

PRACTICING THE RULES

Try filling in the _____. (blanks)

Samples --

I ____ _____ing English.   I **am study**ing English.

He is _____ing at the teacher.   He is **look**ing at the teacher.

The teacher ___ _____ing the class.   The teacher **is teach**ing the class.

She _____ kimchi.   She **eats** kimchi.

∝ ∝ ∝ **Notes** ∝ ∝ ∝

Note here that the action is equal to the time that you want to communicate. Using the verb "be" + ing communicates what you are doing now. Using the "S" without a time word is ok in grammar but is **NOT COMPLETE IN COMMUNICATION.** Using time words is important for the WHOLE idea to be communicated.

∝ ∝ ∝ **Try fixing the problems** ∝ ∝ ∝

My brother is travels to America.   <u>My brother **is** travell**ing** to America</u>

My friend working on the weekend.   _____.

She working at Galleria.   _____.

Do you works at Burger King?   _____.

Does you working tomorrow?   _____.

Are you study English?   _____.

EXERCISE YOUR LEARNING

These sentences are common mistakes in South Korea. They can be understood but can be confusing.

In this exercise you will want to write what is wrong with each sentence. It the problem a COMMUNICATION OF TIME, or does the ACTION NOT FIT the time.

Problem Sentences

1. I wanting lunch for pizza.
2. Where from your house?
3. I am shop for you.
4. Yesterday I will shop for books.
5. Tomorrow I had lunch with you.

What is NOT equal?
Time or Action and Why

Example --

1. **TIME IS NOT EQUAL WITH ACTION**. This is because the "ing" does not communicate the action. This communicates an incomplete idea.

2._____

3._____

4._____

5._____

The Big Fix

Now rewrite the sentences to reflect how you would fix it. The sentence can be longer or shorter but must communicate a complete idea and the action and time **MUST BE EQUAL**.

Example --

I want pizza for lunch today.

2. Where _____ ?

3. I _____ .

4. Yesterday I_____ .

5. Tomorrow I_____ .

Your Turn

Step 1   Listen to your friends when they speak English.
Or, Use your own sentences to do this exercise
(NOT ENGLISH SPEAKERS)

Step 2   Write 5 sentences that sound good to you.

Step 3   Fix them so that EVERYTHING is EQUAL.

❧ ❧ ❧   Notes   ❧ ❧ ❧

Give the students one week to put this together. See if they can pick up the mistakes and correct them. Then review them in class. Give a prize for the most sentences done well.

Body language equals 50% of communication. If this is true then our body language needs to be equal to our words. Use your body to help you communicate what you want, even if you cannot speak the language. If you understand 10% of the speaking and 100% of the body language you will have 60% of communication.

$$10\% = \text{speaking}$$
$$+$$
$$\underline{50\%} = \text{BODY LANGUAGE}$$
$$=$$
$$60\% = \text{✦ } \underline{\textit{Communication}} \text{ ✦}$$

✑ ✑ ✑   NOTES   ✑ ✑ ✑

WE USE BODY LANGUAGE TO COMMUNICATE ACTION.
ACTION WORDS MAKE BODY LANGUAGE.

IN THIS EXERCISE YOU WILL
-- ACT OUT INSTEAD OF SPEAK.
-- PUT A SEQUENCE OF WORDS TOGETHER.
-- COMMUNICATE WHOLE IDEAS
WITHOUT SPEAKING.

Sequence is important. Like the idea from the sentence we used before of having, "lunch for pizza", or "pizza for lunch". Sequence is important. Choosing words to act out first create the core of communication. This is the thinking about what I want to communicate. Building a sequence around it will help the communication become not only better but help understand the idea of whole idea communication.

COMMUNICATE with ACTION

-ACT OUT INSTEAD OF SPEAK.

Choose twelve (12) action words from your list of 100 words and make an action for them.

1. ✦ dance   2. _____   3. _____   4. _____

5. _____   6. _____   7. _____   8._____

9. _____   10. _____   11. _____   12._____

✦ Dance around a bit, close to your desk or in front of the class. Have the class guess what the word is to add some fun to the class activity.

-- PUT A SEQUENCE OF WORDS TOGETHER.

Choose six (6) of these words and make 6 sentences.

Use the **Time/ Action or** Motion/ **Emotion** sequences.

1. **I   like   to dance   before** I go to bed **at night.**
    Emotion   Action   Time   Time

2._____.

3._____.

4._____

5.__ _____

6._____

-COMMUNICATE WHOLE IDEAS WITHOUT SPEAKING.

Write your 6 sentences in a paragraph.
Then use **<u>only</u>** your **body language** to tell the class what you wrote.

_____

_____

_____

_____

_____

_____

_____

෬ ෬ ෬ **Notes** ෬ ෬ ෬

Before starting this exercise inform the students that they will be writing a story. They will need to choose action words that go together.

To help this process make a sequence of time.

Morning / lunch / after lunch / etc.
Start / then / next / / / finally

Then add actions to match the time. Make sentences to reflect this sequence and matching idea.

Morning/ eat rice / then / drive / lunch / order in / ....

THEN ADD EMOTION. A student can do this by moving faster or slower, using their face, or a combination. Have other students write what they see. How accurate is it?

Recap

Write two conversation sequences of three ideas.

Thinking

1. What do I want to **know** in my conversation?
    What do I want to talk or ask about? (topic)

```
1. a. Cars— fast, style, brand, color, drivers, car shows

   b. _____

   c. _____
```

2. What do I want the person to **hear** so I can get a good answer to my question?
    What are good questions to ask?

```
2. a.  What is your favourite car? /   Do you like cars? / _____

   b. _____

   c. _____
```

ℭ ℭ ℭ **Notes** ℭ ℭ ℭ

NOTE that there are three ideas here. A = one idea, and B and C are separate ideas.

BEGINNERS should use easy topics like this one. (*Cars*)
INTERMEDIATE Levels should be more abstract ideas like *Winter Sports*.
HIGH LEVEL could try something like *Careers*.

Writing the Recap Drama

Writing

Example --

Me: Hello, Sam. What is your _**schedule**_ this weekend?

> "_Schedule_" **IS THE BEGINNING TOPIC. It is a good topic to begin a conversation. It is also a question (?) so I can get the response I want.**

Sam: I have nothing planned this weekend. Why do you ask?

> The response or answer plus the question, "Why"? **"Why" helps continue a conversation. "Nothing planned"** leaves the idea open for discussion.

Me: Well, There is a car show in Seoul. Do you want to come with me?

> The answer **changes the topic** to the real topic I want to ask about**? Followed by the question I will get the answer I want to know**.

Sam: Sounds great! What time is it?

> **The answer was a positive response. This is followed by a request for more information in the form of a question.**

Me: It starts at 2:00 on Saturday.
>   Can you meet me at the COEX Mall at 1 o'clock?

The answer is given and one more question?

Sam: Ok. I will meet you. See you Saturday at 2:00.   (Discuss the problem.)

Writing the Recap Drama

Make your own with B or C topics

Write two more conversations. Use the topics you chose for B or C. Find a partner to **WRITE THIS DRAMA** with. When you are finished read it together to **FIX THE SEQUENCE PROBLEMS.** Make sure each _IDEA IS COMPLETE_. **BE PRECISE.** Lazy English is used too often and communication gets mixed up.

TOPIC B - _____

Me:	_____
_____ :	_____
Me:	_____
_____ :	_____
Me:	_____
_____ :	_____
Me:	_____
_____ :	_____
Me:	_____
	_____
Me:	_____
_____ :	_____

🙰 🙰 🙰 Notes 🙰 🙰 🙰

IF THERE IS TIME DO THE SECOND TOPIC. DO NOT STOP AT JUST A FEW LINES. TRY TO EXPAND THE TOPIC AS MUCH AS POSSIBLE. THIS WAY THE STUDENT WILL ACHIEVE MAXIMUM THINKING AND PRACTICE.

Word Challenge
Game

A Vocabulary Making game
where you make it as
easy or hard as you want

WORD CHALLENGE

Getting Ready to Play —

IN THIS GAME I WOULD SUGGEST MAKING OR BUYING A BAG OF LETTERS.

YOU CAN BUY A BAG OR CAN OF LETTERS IN THE KINDERGARTEN OR ELEMENTARY SECTION OF AN EDUCATION BOOKSTORE. I USE A BAG OF LETTERS USED FOR MAKING SPONGE NAMES ON BRACELETS.

STEP 1

Photocopy the grid or make a grid of 25 boxes, or make a grid on the board.

STEP 2

Have each student draw a letter from the bag or box.
Make a total of 10 (ten) maximum

NOTE: More students or larger grids will need more letters to be effective. I have used up to 10 x 10 for a larger class.

STEP 3

Write each letter on the board and have the students suggest words or make words to fit into the box.

ALTERNATE Suggestion for the Board grid

Have the students write their own words to fit the grid. You can limit or expand the game to 3, 4, 5 letter words depending on their vocabulary depth.

Use Lego Instead

1) Buy a box of Lego.

2) Give each team an equal number of blocks.

3) Separate the alphabet into sections of letters, or vowels, verbs, nouns, etc.

4) With each letter taken from the bag the group must place a block for each letter of the word they spell including the small words. If they can make a sentence they can place an extra 10 (ten). Each team needs to build a house.

Who can use ALL the blocks first? Who can build their Project first?

PLAYING THE GAME

STEP 1

Choose a set number of letters larger than 10.im
Make words from these letters.
As many words as you can.
As many letters in one word as you can.

STEP 2

Put them in the boxes below. Put a dot in the boxes you do not use.

The goal of this game is to have NO dots left. There are 25 boxes. Each dot equals (= 1 point). The highest score wins.

The Grid or Game Board Sample

ADIWEJUSIPO

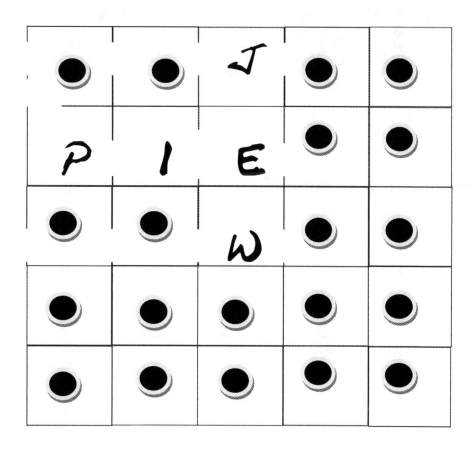

25 - 18 ● = 6   Very Poor

0 - 10 poor   11 - 15 **good**
15 - 20 **very good** 20 - 25 **Genius**

Photocopy the next page if you want to use the grid. I used the white board to play. I had up to four groups at one time. Challenge the teams by giving time limits or larger grids.

BEAT MY SCORE

Put your letters in these boxes

For large groups or higher level groups us a grid of 10x10 and up to 20 letters

Photocopy this page for simple practice

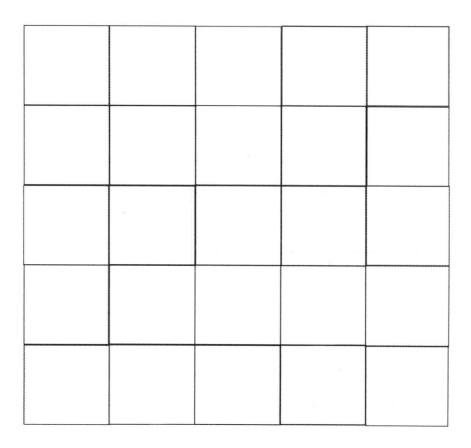

25 - ● = ?

0 - 10 poor   11 - 15 **good**
15 - 20 **very good** 20 - 25 **Genius**

100 More Words

Add more values to your vocabulary

Making sentences longer for Better Communication

Think of 100 more words. These words will help you build the next part of your skills. It is harder, but keep working on this until all the word lines are filled.

AGE

1 young 2_____ 3_____ 4_____ 5_____

6_____ 7_____ 8_____ 9_____ 10 old

11_____ 12_____ 13_____ 14_____ 15_____

16_____ 17_____ 18_____ 19_____ 20_____

21_____ 22_____ 23_____ 24_____ 25_____

SIZE

26_____ 27_____ 28_____ 29 huge 30_____

31_____ 32_____ 33_____ 34_____ 35_____

36_____ 37_____ 38_____ 39 tiny 40_____

41_____ 42_____ 43_____ 44_____ 45_____

46_____ 47_____ 48_____ 49_____ 50_____

♋ ♋ ♋ **Notes** ♋ ♋ ♋

Low — Students at the basic level should be encouraged to use easy words.

Intermediate — Students with this level should use words with more than one syllable at least 50% of the time.

High — Students at this level should use more detailed or combination words for description.

PLACE

51_____   52_____   53_____   54 island   55_____

56_____   57_____   58_____   59_____   60_____

61_____   62_____   63_____   64_____   65_____

66_____   67 coast 68_____   69_____   70_____

71_____   72_____   73_____   74_____   75_____

COLOR

76_____   77_____   78_____   79_____   80_____

81 pink 82_____   83_____   84_____   85_____

86_____   87_____   88_____   89_____   90_____

91 pastel 92_____   93_____   94_____   95_____

96_____   97_____   98_____   99_____   100_____

○३ ○३ ○३ **Notes** ○३ ○३ ○३

These four extra word lists will help communication "be" better. The more description a person can communicate the better.

The Low students should focus on concrete ideas. The higher ones should learn vocabulary. For colors us a pack of crayons to help. For place, look on a map to help get ideas or in books. Use prepositions as much as possible.

100 More Words

Step 1

Choose 1 **word** from each column.   **age/ size/ place/ color**

❶ young / huge / coast / pastel	❷
❸	❹
❺	❻
⑦	⑧

Step 2

Make a **sentence** with all four words.

❶   A **young** couple went to the **huge pastel coast**.
❷
❸
❹
❺
❻
⑦
⑧

Step 3
Choose 1 word from each of the previous 100 words sequence.

time / action / motion / emotion

❶ hour / play / hitting / hard

❷

❸

❹

Step 4
Put all 8 words together.

time / action / motion / emotion / age / size / place / color

❶ hour / play / hitting / hard / young / huge / coast / pastel

❷

❸

❹

- **Have the students choose words that may go together easily.**

- **The first sentence has already been made.**

- **You can change the sentence to reflect the addition of words.**

Step 5

Now make **sentences** to fit these **8** words.

❶   At 5:00 p.m. young men play baseball on the huge pastel coast hitting the ball hard.

Time	age	action		size	color	place	motion	emotion

❷ _____

_____

❸ _____

_____

❹ _____

_____

೫ ೫ ೫ **Notes** ೫ ೫ ೫

This is the conclusion of this section.

There is no right sequence.

> **Each sequence needs to have a**
> > **logical thought pattern to it.**

- **The most important idea first plus time.**
- **The action second.**
- **The second idea last.**
  > **Or**
- **The second idea first.**
- **The action second.**
- **The most important idea last plus time.**

**** The second list requires the use of more prepositions to make it work and should use the past tense form.

*** In Hangul it is the closest structure and will strengthen the use of prepositions for later.

೫ ೫ ೫ **Notes Per Level** ೫ ೫ ೫

Low students need to be encouraged to put their ideas down and then have them corrected.

Intermediate students should **discuss the difference** between **4** words and **8** words.

Which communicates the best and why?

Where AM I?

Making a drama about being lost

Making a drama about a Foreigner being lost

Where Am I?

✦ Asking or giving directions is an important part of first communications in a foreign country.

✦ Learning to ask for or give directions will build on the basic introduction of a conversation.

It will also help with **topic suggestion** and **follow-up thinking**.

Topic — Where **Am I / I Need Help**

GOOD QUESTIONS

Where am I?

I am looking for King Charles Palace, where can I find it?

Is this the right building to find Dunkin Donuts?

Is Dunkin Donuts in this building? (better)

Where can I find a bathroom? (not so good)

How can I get to Saskatoon?

I am lost. I am looking for Joe's Shoes. Do you know where it is?

❦ ❦ ❦ Notes ❦ ❦ ❦

✦ In this chapter you will start to build on the ideas you have already learned. By putting them into a drama the student can/will develop a better thinking pattern and sequence to move beyond an introduction.

✦ When teaching this idea, have the students expand their questions and introductions. Then write the drama as long as possible. Don't stop at the introduction.

The Drama -- Where Am I?

Introduction to the Conversation

Me: Excuse me.
　　　Do you **have a minute**?
Sam: Yes?

Introduction to the Topic

Me: Where **am** I?

Sam: You are in Seoul! (Duh)

Continue the Topic

Me: I know that, but **where** in Seoul?
Sam: Ahh, this is Sadang-dong.

Me: I am looking for Dunkin Donuts,
　　do you know where it **is**?

Sam: I am sorry but I do not know, maybe
the security man would know.

Me: _____

There is a problem with this conversation.
Where is it?
_____

List the **time** words
*Minute*_____

_____

List the **action** words
*know*_____

_____

List the **motion** words
*looking*_____

_____

List the **emotion** words
*Ahhh*_____

_____

ભ ભ ભ **Notes** ભ ભ ભ

This is the beginning of the conversation.

Have the students discuss the time/action/motion/emotion words used and how they affect the communication of the idea, or how using emotion affects the understanding.

The words in black are just a few that need more stress to help understanding. **Are there others?**

57

The Situation - Where Am I?

Situation — You are looking for a shoe store called Suzy Q's. You need to ask someone for help in Saskatoon.

> ## Choose a good question
> ## from "Good Questions" in this chapter and
> ## fill in the lines
> ## with your drama.
> ## Use the Introduction in the left box on the previous page to help you with this exercise.

Example –

Introduction

1. **Me:** Excuse me. Do you **have a minute**?

----- THIS IS A POLITE WAY TO INTRUDE ON SOMEONE'S TIME OR SPACE.

2. **Me:** Excuse me. Do you **have a minute**? **I am lost** and need to find Suzy Q's Shoe Store. Can you help me?

---- *This is an expanded introduction. It asks for a possible intrusion into the other person's time and space, but also gives the reason. If you have a plan it is easier to get a positive response.*

Introduction

3. **Me:** Where **am I**?

----- If you just go around asking, "Where am I?", you will find the response may not be positive because they think you are rude. If you have a map or something people will respond better. Expand the idea like above and have success.

Response

1. **Sam**: *I am sorry I'm busy.*
    (If given a negative pr passive response Sam continues walking without speaking)

2. **Sam**: *Sure! Suzy Q's is one block over.*
    Alternate answer : *I'm sorry I don't know where the shoe store is. Maybe you can ask at the gas station on the corner.*

3. **Sam**: *(no response. Sam continues walking without speaking)*
    Sam with map: *Well, you are here on the map and you want to go there. It's not too hard to find.*

❦ ❦ ❦ **Notes** ❦ ❦ ❦

Sam's response 2 -- Continue this conversation at the gas station. Remember asking good questions will help you get the answer you want.

Sam's response 3 – This conversation is almost over. You have the answer you wanted. Just close with a "thank you" and continue looking. **Ask another person the same question for practice learning to give directions.**

Continue the Topic

Me: _____

Sam: _____

Me: _____

Sam: _____

Me:: _____

Sam: _____

Me: _____

Sam : _____

Situation 2 - Where Am I?

You are on the street and lost.
You were to meet your friend on the corner of 1st Street and Jokers Corner.

You must ❶ _Introduce yourself._
Then you must ❷ _Introduce your problem_ (topic).

Finally you must move to find it.

❸ **Finish the Conversation.**

❧ ❧ ❧ **Notes** ❧ ❧ ❧

Introduction is like an **invitation** to have a **conversation**.

Therefore you need to think of your introduction as an invitation to connect. Think of the situation. In this one you are looking for directions.

Make **different situations** and have students in small teams choose different introductions and follow-up conversation questions and answers. Use a minimum of three questions after initial introduction. Have them write short scripts to the following situations.

Examples –

❶   I want to ask if a Store has a special item I want to buy.

❷   I want to ask someone if I can help them because they look lost.

❸   I just want to ask if you have time for coffee to chat. What would I talk about?

The Method - Where Am I?

Situation

❶   **I want to ask if a Store has a _special item_ I want to buy.**

Good Questions

❶_____

❷_____

❸_____

Me: _____

Sam: _____

Me: _____

Sam: _____

Me: _____

Sam: _____

ଔ ଔ ଔ **Notes** ଔ ଔ ଔ

Finish this on a separate paper if you need. How did you do? Did the student (you) get the information you needed from the questions you asked?

On a separate paper write a script for the other two situations given above.

❷ REVERSE THE SITUATION

I want to ask someone if ***I can help them*** because
they look lost.

Good Questions

❶ _____?

❷ _____?

❸ _____?

Example --

Me: Good morning. You look a bit lost, may I help you?

Sam: Ahhh yes, I am looking for a Burger King. Is there one around here?

Me: _____

Sam: _____

Me: _____

Sam: _____

ಇ ಇ ಇ   Notes   ಇ ಇ ಇ

Notice in this introduction that it is polite. Then the response is polite. Have the students complete a full conversation on a separate page.

Use the good questions to help you. Use one class or more, so that all students have a chance to practice their scripts.

❸ SITUATION

I just want to ask if you have time for coffee to chat.

What would I talk about? (Topics)

How would I introduce the topic I want to chat about?

TOPICS

1. _____

2. _____

3. _____

GOOD QUESTIONS

1. _____

2. _____

3. _____

INTRODUCTIONS

1. _____

2. _____

3. _____

൰ ൰ ൰ Notes ൰ ൰ ൰

Now you have worked on different situations. Finish the conversations so that the student can gain a good understanding of conversations from both sides of a conversation Reverse ideas change the questions a little and is an important part of this exercise.

1+1+___ =?

A conversation with more than two people

Conversation Rhythm

A conversation with MORE THAN two

Many times you meet someone but you can't get past hello. You didn't memorize enough or you didn't develop your skill enough.

LET'S TRY TO GO ONE MORE STEP.

PROBLEM

Often when you meet someone your brain forgets what to do next. So you blurt out some memorized form of conversation.

IMAGINE THIS —

You have learned some new phrases in English class and are now meeting some other people.

Practice this together **and then in** groups of three.

Hello: How U doin'?
    Me 2: Great and you?
Hello: My name is Hello! What's yours?
    Me 2: Me 2.
Hello: Really?
    Me 2: Yes, and this is my friend Really.
Really: Nice to meet you. Really!
    Hello: Me 2. What are you doing today with Really?
Me 2: Well, I would like to go for coffee.
    Hello: Really! How about you?
Really: Well, I will just follow Me 2.

Sounds silly I know.

What is the problem with this conversation?
Are there any new phrases?

REVIEW

.... the sequence

Make a question (Q) — answer the question (A) —

What does the third person do or say?

Question — Answer — **?** — Question — Answer — **?**

❧ ❧ ❧ Notes ❧ ❧ ❧

The sequence remains the same but the third presents a problem. Discuss the idea of what does the third person say or do. Do they just say, "ok"? How does the question change? Do you just ask "and you"?

Three or more people change the conversation a little but not a lot. It takes more work to include the other people. It takes some repetition with a small twist.

In this exercise the students should introduce a third person, or be introduced to a third or more party. I put my students in teams of 4 to do this introducing each other as a friend of the other. You can do this in 3 + 1 or 2 + 2, etc.

In a conversation, when you first meet someone, use their name when you ask them questions. This will help you remember them.

In a conversation, ask questions which will give you information (thinking rule #1). If you ask "Do..." questions you will get a yes or no answer. So use the name first and then ask about their relationship or job.

Problem — In Korea too many children and people ask for name and country but never go farther. This is because information questions are just memorized. This can sometimes be thought of as rude. If this happens a few times it is ok. But because it happens too often it is considered rude.

Solution --- Asking about a relationship to your friend or their relationship to you is better and takes more thinking time.

LET US GET STARTED

Situation – Two friends are meeting at Starbucks Coffee. One friend is bringing a friend who does NOT know the other.

BIG BUCKS COFFEE SHOP

S1: Hello. Q – Sam! Who did you bring with you?

S2: A -- Hi John! This is my friend Sue. Sue this is my friend John.

S1: Hi Sue, Q -- _____

ભ   ભ   ભ   ભ   ભ   ભ   ભ   ભ   ભ

TEACHERS — Questions should be made so that a short response can be made and then a new question to a new student.

Respond with words like –That's great, Terrific, Wonderful, That's too bad, Oh, no! You're kidding, Oh, really. I see, etc.

Use them **only once**.

– STAY AWAY FROM THE STANDARD Q'S LIKE, "What's your name?"

How many different good questions can we think about to ask Sue in the dialogue above?

1. _____

2. _____

3. _____

4. _____

5. _____

Many times you meet someone
but they or you have a friend.

How you introduce or ask about this friend is important.

Example --

Asking about their friend~~

   ❶ Who is he/she?
     or
   ❶ Who is your friend?

   ❷ What does your friend do?

Introducing your friend~~

   ❶ This is my friend _____. (Sue)
  or
   ❶ This is _____ my friend. (Sue)
  or
   ❶ I'd like you to meet my friend. _____ this is John. (Sue)

Example --

                                Q= question   A =Answer

S1: Hello. Q – Sam! Who did you bring with you? ❶

S2: A -- Hi John! This is my friend Sue. ❶   Sue this is my friend John. ❶

S1: Hi Sue, Q -- What does your friend do? ❷

∽ ∽ ∽ **Notes** ∽ ∽ ∽

Discuss the following questions. Then discuss what "Sue" would say next. Write a couple of examples and complete the conversation at Big Bucks Coffee Shop.

LET US CONTINUE THE CONVERSATION

Which is the best of each?

I have put a ❶ for the best to use above. **Asking** has a ❷ and I would recommend that as a second question.

Which ones do you use most in your own language or culture?

_____

How does this compare with **how YOU use English**?

_____

How often do you have to introduce your friend to someone else?

_____

S1: Hello. Q – Sam! Who did you bring with you?

S2: A -- Hi John! This is my friend Sue. Sue this is my friend John.

S1: Hi Sue, Q -- What does your friend do?

S3: I am an Executive Assistant at Kwando Motors.
        Q – How long have you known Sam?

S1: A - _____ Q-- _____

Change the topic now by <u>asking a better question</u>.

෬ ෬ ෬ **Notes** ෬ ෬ ෬

It is easy to change a topic. Just ask a question which requires an answer in a different direction.

You can keep control of a conversation by using good questions. Changing conversation topics is not considered rude if you use good questions.

Be Aware of HOW you say things

Use Mr., Mrs., Dr., or other titles only when necessary. It is a show of respect but it can also be a negative. Using titles can be important to the person but if used wrong can show the lack of respect shown in a relationship.

Children should be taught to use Mr. and Mrs., plus the last name.

Adults to Adults should use it as a general rule. If you add more than the Surname you express your attitude about the person.

ଔ   ଔ   ଔ   ଔ   ଔ   ଔ   ଔ   ଔ   ଔ

Let's introduce your friend first

You are introducing your friend to another person in your social group.

-- A Social group is a group of people you hang out or socialize with.

You — Hey Bob!
    Bob!
    Bob.   This is *John,*   my friend   from <u>School</u>.
               This is *John*   a   buddy   from <u>Work</u>.
               This is *John*   a Business Associate
               This is *John*   an old friend   from my <u>home town</u>.

Who you are talking with	*Who* you are *Introducing?*	What **relationship** they are to you	What <u>connection</u> they are to the situation

ଔ   ଔ   ଔ   **Notes**   ଔ   ଔ   ଔ

Most people introduce the third person or more in a social situation. It does not have to be a long conversation but should answer the four (4) questions above so that everyone in the group can understand how to talk to them later.

Let's Ask about Your Friend's friend

✦ You — Hey Bob!
　　　Bob!
　　　Bob.　**Who is your friend? (best)**
　　　　　　Is that someone from work/ your office? **(a bit rude)**
　　　　　　What's your friend's name?　**(polite)**
　　　　　　Who is that person with you? (if the person is not beside - **polite)**
　　　　　　Who did you bring with you? **(just information not interest)**

You Try It

Write four (4) situations that <u>you have</u>, **or** <u>think you will find yourself in</u>, to introduce yourself to another person who is with a person you know.

1._____

2._____

3._____

4._____

Situation -- 1
　　　　　　　　You are bringing your friend to meet another.

Me:_____

Sue: _____

Friend: _____

_____:_____ _____

_____:_____

_____:_____

_____:_____

71

Situation -- 2

You are meeting your friend who has a surprise friend.

Me:_____

Sue: _____

Friend: _____

_____:_____

_____:_____

_____:_____

_____:_____

SITUATION -- 3

- -

Me:_____

Sue: _____

Friend: _____

_____:_____

_____:_____

_____:_____

_____:_____

൙ ൙ ൙ **Notes** ൙ ൙ ൙

✦Did you ask good questions?

✦ ✦Did you get the answer you wanted to your questions introduction?

✦ ✦ ✦Now write the rest of the conversation on a separate piece of paper, or use the bottom of this page.

Steak and Potatoes

Visualizing conversation
To improve
Listening skills

Steak and Potatoes

If you are a teacher it is important to teach so that your students **visualise what you teach.** The title to this part is about understanding the words that are primary, or most important.

Steak and Potatoes is one way to do this. Imagine a meal at a restaurant. It has many pieces. Each piece or part of the meal is very tasty. But each part also makes the presentation more attractive to the customer.

If we study grammar as just rules we will find all the pieces to a great meal. But, if we learn how to cook them into a great menu we improve our enjoyment in making it (using our vocabulary which grows), and the joy of others understanding and appreciating the effort it takes to present it.

Steak words are the key focus of a full sentence.

In conversation we often make full sentences short. By learning which are the steak words, we can understand which words to cut out and which words are important. If we take out the wrong words we do communicate what we want.

Write down some words. They need to be 4 or 5 letters long. They should be nouns or topic words.

STEAK WORDS

1 _SOCCER___ 2 _____ 3 _____ 4 _____

5 _____ 6 _____ 7 _____ 8 _____

Potato words

—These are words that add to the idea. They are important and may be used as an object of a sentence. These are **NOT** adjectives.

1 _____ 2 __BALL____ 3 _____ 4 _____

5 _____ 6 _____ 7 _____ 8 _____

LET US CONTINUE THE MEAL

Write down some words to help the Steak and Potatoes.

I call these GARNISH. They are small words which help the other words work together.

Garnish words

1 __like____ 2 _____ 3 ___a_____ 4 _____

5 _____ 6 __blue____ 7 _____ 8 _____

9 _____ 10 _____ 11 _____ 12 _____

13 _____ 14 _____ 15 _____ 16 ___the____

Put it together

Step 1

_____

_____

Example --

Steak = soccer
Potato = ball
Garnish = like, blue, the

∽ ∽ ∽ **Notes** ∽ ∽ ∽

Have the students choose words that go together. All the words should compliment the steak word.

Step 2

Put them in a line.

Soccer ball like blue the.

Does this make sense? **OF COURSE NOT.**

Are there enough words to make sense? **maYBe!**

Do we need to add words or change words? **Yes / No**

Change **words?**

Which words would you change?
the Steak   the Potato   or   the Garnish?

_Why would you change it or them?_____

Add **words?**

Which words would you add?

More Potato   or   more Garnish?

✦ *Why would you add it or them?*

❧ ❧ ❧ **Notes** ❧ ❧ ❧

Changing words is possible for all three because the choice of words may make it hard to work with. Adding words is limited to only the two choices because steak words are the focus point. **Adding words will give more detail to the steak. I would focus on more garnish words if the students want to add them.**

Finishing the idea

DIFFERENT COMBINATIONS

SAMPLE WORDS LIST — *Soccer ball like blue the.*

❶ The soccer blue like ball

❷   The blue soccer ball like

❸   The blue like soccer ball

❹   Ball like blue the soccer

The options are endless but *we do __not need__ to add or change any of the words.*

✦ Which one of the lines of words is a good idea?

A good idea is an idea that communicates what we want.

✦ Remember good grammar is not enough.

WE NEED TO COMMUNICATE SOMETHING.

The blue like soccer ball ......

∝ ∝ ∝ **Notes** ∝ ∝ ∝

This seems simple, but many students do not choose words that match. Which ever words are chosen do not change for the student. This is important because the student at this point must put his words together to communicate. Discovering the best fit in communication can take some time. Do not rush this time. Discuss the ideas with the student or class so all can learn from this exercise. When this section is finished move on to complete the idea using time / action or motion / emotion words.

Step 3

Add some action with another potato word.

The blue like soccer ball was kicked by me.

Steak		Action + Time	Garnish + Potato

Now you have a good sentence that has all the elements of <u>good communication.</u>

Now you have better understanding of the idea you may want to change them. Look at your STEAK, POTATO, and GARNISH words. Do you want to change any now?

Change them now.

෴ ෴ ෴ **Notes** ෴ ෴ ෴

✦ The STEAK word is the center or key word. In our example Soccer was the key idea. Everything else focussed on it.

✦ The POTATO words are only one or two to explain the soccer idea like ball and blue.

✦ The GARNISH words help me understand the time and action of what you want to communicate. These small words are needed to help me understand the WHOLE idea.

You do not cook without spices, and you do not use only STEAK words to communicate well. The better you communicate, the better the conversation, the less stress and more confidence.

Step 4

Take one ❶ STEAK word + two ❷ Potato words + three ❸ GARNISH words and put them in a line.

❶ ❷ ❷ ❸ ❸ ❸

Now change them into a reasonable idea.

___ ___ ___ ___ ___ ___

Now add words to finish the idea like **Step 3**

___ ___ ___ ___ ___ ___

___ ___ ___

How does it look? *Do this again, on a separate page, for good practice.*

Use ALL the words You wrote in the three categories

ଔ ଔ ଔ **Notes** ଔ ଔ ଔ

✦ The student wrote 8 steak and potato words, plus 16 garnish words in an earlier exercise. Go back to these words and have them practice putting them into communication ideas, until all the words have been used.

✦ Practicing how words go together to communicate is important. **Often the grammar is ok, but communication is not.** Most of the time you need to **change the order of the words not the words themselves.** Using more garnish will add to the communication level.

This is like a baked potato, or a potato with bacon bits, sour cream, and chives, topped with cheddar cheese, steak alone, or steak with a marinade mushroom sauce.

✦ Use discussion with the student so the student will choose the words and make all the changes for maximum learning.

REAL PRACTICE

Use the sentences you have made to make a conversation. Do this in a team so you can communicate your ideas in a conversation format.

Example --
—- The sentence we made ---

The blue like soccer ball was kicked by me.

Abe: Hello John!
John: Hello Abe! How are you doing?

Abe: I am doing ok. How about you?
John: Well, I am in a little bit of trouble.

Abe: How come?
John: Well, I was playing with a friend in the park and a soccer ball broke a car window.

Abe: Really?
John: Yes. They said that I have to pay for the window. It was the color of the ball that we were playing with that was the problem.

Abe: How terrible!

John: Yes! **The blue like soccer ball was kicked by me,** but it was not our ball that broke the window. I feel terrible. My mother will be very angry.

∝ ∝ ∝ **Notes** ∝ ∝ ∝

✦ Use what the student has learned already in this book. Introductions first and then **set up the story for the sentence to be used.**

✦ Have the students discuss and write ideas /stories that they can use their sentences in. Then have them write the conversation on a separate piece of paper. Use two ~ four students in a team. The more students in the group the longer the conversation will be.

Star Vocabulary

A game where you make stars with vocabulary

Star Vocabulary

Step 1 — Make a set of boxes so they look like a star

Step 2 — In the center box put a consonant

Step 3 — Around the consonant put the vowels
(A,E,I,O, U, - y)

Step 4 — Make words starting from the
CENTER LETTER to the outside

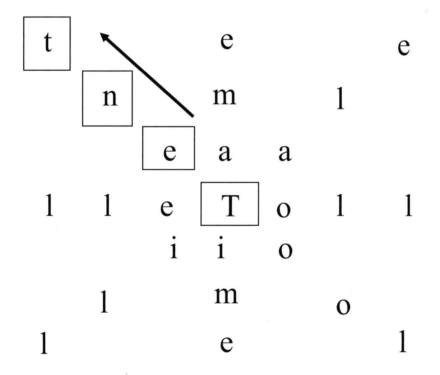

a	e	i

		o		o		

i	a	u

**Try different letters in the center to test your
vocabulary
and become a STAR**

Time Travel

Time words
To help us
communicate better

A POINT IN TIME MAKES YOUR ENGLISH CLIMB.

ᑫ ᑫ ᑫ **Notes** ᑫ ᑫ ᑫ

✦ When you have a conversation you need to communicate a time.

✦ A **time** to do an action.

✦ A **time** to make a reference to.

✦ In English writing **you need to let the person who is reading know a time to think about.**

✦ **Time is not always spoken** but if you do it will help you communicate better.

Refer to the first 100 word list you did before.

What words can be used to help understand **time**?

Thinking

When do you _____? (action)

What **time** do you _____?(action)

Tell me a time when _____(action)

How **often** _____?(action)

I study **from** _____ to _____(time)

I made _____(action)

I **am** driving _____(direction/place/ etc.)

_____

87

෬ ෬ ෬ **Notes** ෬ ෬ ෬

✦ Grammar is about understanding time values. It is not just an ending or Something to memorize. *I highlighted the time related words or letters in the example on the previous page.*

✦ It is about communicating the time of an action or event. This is one of the most important ideas to understand.

When you communicate time everything else will be understood most of the time.

Let's check it out.

Example --

There is a barbeque.

What information is missing?

What information do you need to know to understand what I want to tell you?

Write your answer as a QUESTION.

A. _____?

B. _____?

෬ ෬ ෬ **Notes** ෬ ෬ ෬

✦ If you used the words (when) time or (where) place, you are right. We need these words to be understood.

✦ If you do **NOT** know the time of an event the conversation will give you stress.

Good Grammar is NOT ALWAYS good Communication

I want to go fishing.

I have a birthday.

> Do these have **good grammar**?   Yes   No
> Do these have **good communication**?   Yes   No

✦ Basically the sentences have good grammar and communication. The missing information is time. Going fishing or having a birthday will demand more questions. More questions demand more answers.

✦ Now we will fix these sentences so that there is a time element in them.

✦ Read them out loud and see if they feel different, or communicate the idea better.

Let's fix these sentences **so they communicate what we want.**

I want to go fishing **on Sunday**.
I have a birthday **on July 4th**.

Time word to note is "**ON**".

✦ We think of "**on**" as "on top of" something.

✦ It is a **position word** linked with a time word.

Adding Time

Mark on a calendar these two dates, *Sunday and July 4th.*

- I want to go fishing.   *I have a birthday.*

Both have good grammar, but **when** should you do this? *Are they the same time?*

Let's add some **time words** to our vocabulary.

Example --

Now, later, soon, never, sometime, future, past, week, weekend, day (Sunday....), o'clock, minute (s), seconds, hour (s), a.m., p.m., afternoon, morning, evening, night, noon, then, as soon as, for the time being, schedule, routine, continue, _____,

_____, _____

෬ ෬ ෬ Notes ෬ ෬ ෬

We have many time words. **But _ALL_ time words must fit the endings or use of words.** When we use "now" we need to use the other words like "is", because both have the same *time* value.

✦ Learning to use words together helps us **communicate better**.

✦ Learning to use words together helps **improve our writing skills**.

෬ ෬ ෬

Make this connection so you can learn words that go together.

Now   --- I am + ___ing, is, make, give to,

Past   ---   _____

Future   ---   _____

After   ---   _____, _____, _____

Before ---   _____, _____, _____

Communicating Time

✦ When we talk about schedule we use the word "**plan**".

✦ When we use the word routine we use the word "**at**".

✦ Schedule is about a **future time**.

✦ Routine is about a **daily action**.

Working it out

Now use your new time words and connections to make a conversation.

Example --

Me: Hello! How are you doing today?
> **You**: I'm doing great! What are you doing this weekend?

Me: I'm going to go fishing on Saturday? What about you?
> **You**: Well, I think I will go to a movie Saturday night.

Look how many **time** words and **connections** we have used already.

Time IS IMPORTANT

Now let's take the time words away.

Hello! How are you doing?
> I' doing great! What you do this?
I' to go fish? What about you?
> Well, I think I go to a movie.

How much do you understand now compared to the first example?

91

Learning to use words together

Repetition — *this means to repeat many times. In a conversation it will help you if you **repeat what you hear.** This helps the person confirm you have heard right.*

ℭ ℭ ℭ **Notes** ℭ ℭ ℭ

✦ In this exercise use what the student has learned about introductions, topic building, good questions, etc. Focus the use of time words to complete the ideas.

✦ This is a step by step plan. The student needs to have a topic to talk about. Then develop questions about the topic. Finally the student will use the answers to the questions to make the conversation.

Choosing the Topic

What topics do you want to talk about in your introduction?

❶ _____   ❷ _____

| Topic ❶ _____ |

What questions can you ask about this topic? Write five (5) questions.

1._____?

2._____?

3._____?

4._____?

5._____?

| Topic ❷ _____ |

What questions can you ask about this topic? Write five (5) questions.

1._____?

2._____?

3._____?

4._____?

5._____?

CR   CR   CR

Step 1

Add the questions and then give answers in the following conversation.

Step 2

Underline the TIME words. Use the next page to finish the conversation.

Step 3 **Read** the dialogue you made with your partner. Us as much expression or body
        language as possible.

Me: Hello! How are you doing today?

                    You: I'm doing great! What are you doing this weekend?

Me: I'm going to go fishing on Saturday? What about you?

                    You: Well, I think I will go to a movie Saturday night.

_____

                    _____

_____

                    _____

_____

                    _____

_____ _____

                          _____

_____ _____

_____ _____

  _____ _____

_____ _____

_____ _____

_____ _____

_____ _____

_____ _____

_____ _____

_____ _____

_____ _____

_____ _____

_____

CR CR CR

NOW LET'S TRY SPEAKING AND ACTING.

✦✦ _Stress **ALL** **THE UNDERLINED WORDS.**_

A Point in Time

Small words
that
help communicate
Time

A Point in Time

✦ <u>Time</u> words go together with <u>action</u> words. If you learn to use them together your communication will be much better. **Understanding** words that are equal (=) help you **listen** better as well.

✦ **Position** words do not go well together with **action** words side by side. You need to use words that help understand **action** and **position** together.

✦ ✦ "**Do**" is used to ask for agreement in the answer. So you answer **yes** or **no**.

> "**Do**" is a small word but very important. We use it a lot because the answer is simple, but many times the question is asking for more. Let's look at this a bit.

"**Do**" is also asking for an **ACTION** answer.

Example --

Do you travel?   **Answer = yes, or no.**

Do you travel?   **Yes! I do.**

What information was given here?   Lots   Some   None

Does your answer help your conversation? _____

Do you travel?
            Yes! I **do,** and you**?**
                    Yes! I love to travel.

Travel is an action word **but not enough** to continue a conversation.

❧ ❧ ❧ **Notes** ❧ ❧ ❧

✦ Look back at the answers given to the question, "**Do you travel**?" The first answer is a *basic easy answer* because the question was a *basic easy question*. The second answer adds emotion (**love**) to it. This extra word helps the other person want to ask more questions like, Where/ Which/ When/ Who/ etc.

✦ In this section you will consider the value of the word "**do**". "**Do**" has a different value when it is positioned differently in the sentence.

❧ ❧ ❧

Rule # 1

..... Of conversation is that you must have a question and answer rhythm.

Do = Action

Example --

What do you **do** <u>on</u> holidays?

Say these sentences with the stress on the **second do**. "**do**" in the <u>middle</u> of a sentence **requires an *ACTION* answer.**

What do you **do** <u>on</u> **holidays**?

What do you **do** <u>in</u> your **free time**?

❧ ❧ ❧

The English Math Rule

"**Do**?" + **a point in time = action word answer.**

97

Rule # 2

What you want the _other person to hear_
you stress.

DO + TIME

When "**do**" is positioned before a **_time word_**, the answer is not, YES or NO, because of this position. **THE ANSWER SHOULD BE AN ACTION WORD.**

Example --

Holidays is a point in time.

> **Free time is _NOT_** a point in time so we use **in**.

SAY THE SENTENCES AGAIN WITH THE STRESS AND IT IS
> _easy to hear and_
> **+** _easy to understand what you want._

Now do it again with the "do" words changing places. Which one is better and easier to hear and understand?   ❶   or   ❷
❶   or   ❷

❶   What **do** you do **on holidays**?

> **❷**   What do you **do on** holidays?

❶   What **do** you do **in** your **free time**?

> **❷**   What do you **do** _in your_ **free time**?

☙ ☙ ☙ Notes ☙ ☙ ☙

✦There are a couple things to note here. The first is to rephrase the sentence. This will help discover if what is understood. The second is the difference between **on** and **in.** "You" comes **before** the second "do" with "on'. The change to "your" comes **after** the "do".

IN ------ SPACE, A PLACE, OR TIME

A box has a beginning and an end. So "in" is a **long word** *not* a **point word**.

When we talk about something — *in* — we can think of a *point that is* **between** two **connected other points**.

a place to do an action

    IN ~ **a mall, office, classroom, water**

Each set of points is an "in" idea.
    Make one **sentence** or **question** with "in".

Let's try it

• Hello! What are you doing **in** the mall?

    • I was shopping **in** the shoe store. What are you doing?

• Well! I am **in** the classroom looking for my books. Can you come help me?

    • I don't know. I don't think I can make it **in** time.

• How about **in** July? Would you have time then?

    • Yes, **in** July is better.

Make a conversation ~ ❶ choose a topic to ask about ❷ reply with "**in**".

_____

_____

_____

_____

At — the moment in time

"**at**" is used for *a point in time and place*.

At this moment .... — **A nice song by Celine Dion.**

"**At**" is a very **specific** time or place.

      --- If you use a place you must **add a noun and an article (a, the).**
        --- If you use it for time you need to give it **an exact time.**

Example --

✦   I like to swim **at the** pool **at** 6 o'clock

✦ ✦   I left my beach towel back at **the** house **on the** beach.

෴ ෴ ෴ Notes ෴ ෴ ෴

✦   Here we use both **at** and **on**. "**At**" to tell us where the house is exactly. "**On**" to help us understand where the house is.

    --- **On** helps us understand that the house is *__closer to the beach__* than **at** does.
    --- **At** tells us that the house is *__in the area of the beach__*.

    --- **On** is a general position word**.**
       Get __on__ with it means to move in a direction. (Any direction)

    --- **On** is used for position *not a point*.
    --- **On** is sometimes used like **at** for general place or position**.**

Example --

Put the box *__on__* **the** table.   (Anywhere on the table is a general position)
Put the box *__on the__* **corner** of the table**.**

Use these words like on, at, in to finish this sentence.

This summer I will _____

Do it on time

Think about the holidays in your Country.

How many can you list with their dates?

Use **on** and **in** to help you tell about **time**.

EXAMPLE —

July 1 — Canada Day

On July 1 celebrate Canada Day. **In** the morning I sing "O Canada" and **in** the afternoon we dance **in** the street. **In** the evening some people drink Red Beer. I hope this year it is **on** a Friday.

On = a BIG BOX
In = a TIME BOX

௸ ௸ ௸ Notes ௸ ௸ ௸

Writing

On the previous page you had a sentence about summer activity. In this section the focus on using in, at, and on will be used. These are key time and place words. Encourage the students write not only a sentence but a paragraph.

Conversation

This is a move now to writing skills practice. If you want to continue the conversation making, have the students write them on a separate sheet using what they have learned about good questions using in, at, and on in their answers.

Review Writing

Step 1

List the holidays or special days in one year.
Give their dates (time)

Name	Date

Example --

New Years Day   **On** January 1 (USA)

_____   _____
_____   _____
_____   _____
_____   _____
_____   _____
_____   _____
_____   _____

Adding Action

What do **you** DO that is special **(action)**

Now add the words at / on / in to complete the sentence. Then make your own.

July 1/ Canada Day – **Sing** O Canada/ **Dance** in the Street/ **Drink** Red Beer

On July 1, Canada Day, I **Sing** O Canada, **Dance in** the Street, and **Drink** Red Beer.

_____

What **emotions** do you have on these special days?

Sad/ Happy/Excited/ .....

_____

_____

Step 2

Write a paragraph about this special day using the words you have learned.

Example --

On July 1, I <u>sing</u> "O Canada", <u>drink</u> red beer, and <u>dance</u> **in** the street. **In** the evening I <u>watch</u> the fireworks in the sky. I feel <u>happy</u> for my country. I feel <u>sad</u> because of the economy. I feel <u>excited</u> because it is a holiday for me.

_____

_____

_____

_____

_____

_____

Read this to the class when you are finished.

Better Vocabulary
Better Communication

Remember the vocabulary on emotional value. The **more vocabulary you can learn with these values, the** **Better** **your communication.**

Vocabulary Challenge

Write your **action words** on one line and add (+) words that have the **same action.**

Example --

Sing = chant, yell   _____ _____ _____ _____

Dance = jump, swing, shuffle _____ _____ _____ _____

Drink = guzzle, sip, gulp   _____ _____ _____ _____

Watch = _____ _____ _____ _____

Write your **emotion words** on one line and add (+) words that have the same **emotion value.**

Example --

Sad = remorseful, unhappy   _____ _____ _____ _____

Happy = energetic, jovial   _____ _____ _____ _____

Excited = exuberant, giggly, nervous   _____ _____ _____ _____

_____ = _____ _____ _____ _____

Step 3

Fill in the blanks with **different** WORDS.

On July 1, I _____ "O Canada", _____, and _____

in the street. In the evening I _____ the fireworks in the sky. I feel

_____ for my country. I feel _____ because of the economy.

I feel _____ because it is a holiday for me.

ଦ୍ଥ ଦ୍ଥ ଦ୍ଥ **Notes** ଦ୍ଥ ଦ୍ଥ ଦ୍ଥ

Go back to the 100 words pages. Use the emotion words you put there if you need help. You can do the same for actions. In this exercise have the student use two or three different holidays and use different action and emotion words in each. You may need to encourage them to use their imagination. It will seem hard and may need a lot of encouragement. Work in teams may be help them work it out.

ଦ୍ଥ ଦ୍ଥ ଦ୍ଥ

Write a paragraph using the **Time, Action, and Emotion** words. **Use as many as possible.**

_____

_____

_____

_____

One more time with a different day.

_____

_____

Do these extra words **help** you communicate better? Why?

_____

_____

_____

_____

_____

Do these words **help** your writing, speaking, or **both**? _____

How do they **help** you?

Give some examples of how the words **can help** or **hinder** your **writing or speaking.**

_____

_____

_____

_____

_____

_____

_____

ભ ભ ભ **Notes** ભ ભ ભ

Many students are too shy to interact at this level. Encourage them to write first if speaking is a problem. Then they can read their answers. There are NO right or wrong answers here. There are just personal views both negative and positive.

Small Words Count

**Small words
are
what make communication
smooth**

Small WORDS COUNT

Small words are important because they tell us position or direction. They also tell us distance close or far. They can also tell us what we need to add to help our communication be better. Remember that good communication in English is about using Time, Action, Motion (ing), and Emotion words.

Let's find out how this works so we can use them better in our conversation.

Action / Motion

From — **POSITION** — start point of action
                    (Action)

Inside — **POSITION** — **CLOSE**
                    (Motion — you move something from outside to inside)

Toward — **DIRECTION** — **CLOSE**
                    (Motion — you move something closer to an object)

CR   CR   CR

In this exercise the student wants to do several things.

❶   For each word write **- position** or **direction**. Understanding this idea will help the student to communicate their ideas better.

❷   For each word write **- action** or **motion**. An action is defined as just an action. It does not imply motion. Motion is defined by an inference to action.

❸   With each word write a reason why you chose the idea you did.

Let's Try It Together

Example~~

Around — **position** — **motion** -- (Around is position because it is on the <u>outside of something</u>. It is ***motion*** because we use it mostly with the action "***go***" or "***move***" and often includes space)

Across — _____ — _____ -- (_____

_____)

Beneath — _____ — _____ -- (_____

_____)

By means of — _____ — _____ -- (_____

_____)

Except for — _____ — _____ -- (_____

_____)

Apart from — _____ — _____ -- (_____

_____)

Concerning — _____ — _____ -- (_____

_____)

With — _____ — _____ -- (_____

_____)

Was this difficult? If it was you are very normal. Isn't that exciting?

✦ When you learn to think of these small words as **MORE THAN JUST WORDS**, but

IMPORTANT COMMUNICATION POINTS,

YOU WILL COMMUNICATE BETTER.

൙ ൙ ൙ Notes ൙ ൙ ൙

✦ If students have trouble with this exercise, have them make sentences with them to discover what they do. Asking students to consider what these small words communicate will help their thinking skills.

✦ **Understanding** what these words communicate will help improve the students understanding of their everyday use.

✦ **Writing out** the reasons for their choices will help them, not only process their ideas, but create a stronger link in their memory for later use.

✦ **Discuss** how these words are used in their native language, if your students are intermediate or higher. This discussion of their language use will help them understand the values and use better. Often we do not think about why we use these words. Understanding the "why" will help us understand how to correct and improve our communication.

✦ Remember that we have considered the idea that time words and action words should go together. The next exercise will look at more small words that help connect ideas together, adding contrast or give a limit to the idea or action.

Small **Words** = **Big Communication**

Contrast or Limitation

Negative but Positive
Yes   but   No

-- The word "but" tells the person listening to you that there is a change.

- Communicating this word is like a stop and go in different directions. It is a direct contrast or gives a limitation to the idea you are communicating.

But = *an **opposite value** to what has gone before.*

ભ ભ ભ **Notes** ભ ભ ભ

✦ Use **But** + a **small word** in one sentence.

✦ Use the small words to give you a time, an action, some motion, or an emotion value

Example — Since, instead of, as for, in case

Since I study English I can find a better job, **but** **instead of** studying I chose a lower paying job. **As for** my promotions, I think the next job will have to be a higher paying job, **in case** I want to have career.

ભ ભ ભ

Let's Try It Together

--- As the example shows, use 4 ~ 5 small words plus but to make a story or paragraph.

--- Notice in the example some small words need partner words like **of, for, or in**, to communicate better.

Choose a few **<u>small words</u>** to use — _____

Now make a sentence or paragraph with all of them.

_____

_____

_____

The Almost Complete List of Small Words

About *above* according to *after* against *along* along with
among *as* **as for** *at* because of *before* behind *below*
beside *between* beyond **but*** by *despite* down *during*
except *excepting* for *in* in addition **to** in back *of* in case of
in front *of* in place of in spite *of* into like near next *of*
off on *onto* on top of out out of outside over past
regarding round **<u>since</u>** through throughout till to under
underneath unlike until up upon up **to** within without

ભ   ભ   ભ

NOTE: "Of" used together with other words = motion

"To" used together with other words = action **of object**

✦ ✦ **Use the Let's Try It Together** words to make them into sentences using the same values.

THE SMALL WORDS DRAMA

Use the sentences you have just made and make a conversation with them.

You want to have a discussion about studying English and finding a job with two other friends, SAM and SUE.

Topic — Study English

Good Questions?

1. Why_____?

2. How _____?

3. When _____?

4. Where_____?

5. What _____?

Introduction

Me: Hello Sam! How are you doing today?

    Sam: I'm going ok. How about you?

Me: Well! English is hard for me. How is the English class for you Sue?

    Sue: I think it is hard, but it is also a lot of fun. The games are not so hard.

Sam: You are right. But it is still hard for me. I am so busy.

(Use your questions and answers to finish the conversation. A page is provided after the Step by Step Instructions page.)

Step by Step Instructions for the Drama Game

This game is designed to give students a combination of fun and learning. Using small words can be hard to understand. Memorizing them is not so difficult. Using them in real life is hard because in Hangul they are not used, or they are translated with so many other ideas.

·· So the **fun** is the game. ·· The *learning* is putting them in a sequence that makes sense. Therefore there needs to be a discussion with each sentence to make sure it fits. Remember that conversation is a combination of Questions and Answers about ideas. Each sentence should fit the idea. Adding more is OK. The longer the drama the better.

STEP 1

Make sure each student has a playing piece to start. Each student should also choose an English name. In the Drama they will need to write their name.

STEP 2

The beginning of the drama is written for you. Write ***Sam:*** _____ on the board as high as possible. Have one student start by rolling the die. The student will move the number on the die and do the action.

STEP 3

Write the sentence or idea on the board to fit the drama sequence. If it is a question ask another student to give an answer to write under it. The next student should write a question.

Be sure to use the names the students have chosen. The students will write the sentences on their own paper.

When half the students have reached the finish line stop the game.

THE SMALL WORDS DRAMA
Basic Rules How to Play

1. Make the die (**pattern can be found on the next page**) and follow the directions on it and move the number of spaces it shows.

2 If you are at a ladder you can move up / down by **creating a conversation using small words.** A conversation is made up of two or more people.

Question *and Answer* = 1 spot on the ladder.

You must climb the WHOLE ladder by conversation or return to where you started and lose a turn. It can be a nice short cut.

3. If you cannot make a sentence **you lose one turn**.

4. **You must do the instructions** for each box or die (dice)

5. The winner is the first one through to the end.

6. To begin try rock / paper / scissors.

7. Markers can be spots or you can use anything else you prefer.

8. **You cannot use the same small word from the list twice in one sentence.**

9. **If you stop on the ladders going up you <u>must</u> go up the ladder.**

Write the sentences from the game on a paper or the white/black board to finish this conversation. If you need to change the topic **make a transition sentence or a question.**

Make the Dice

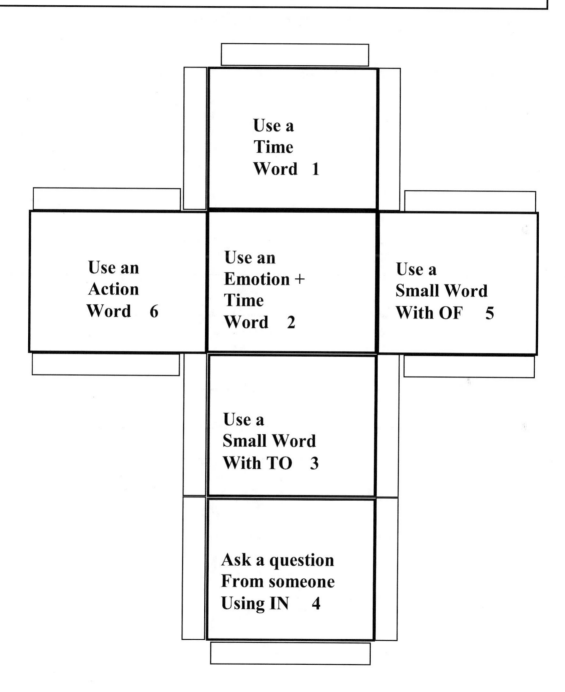

**** **Use heavy paper or stiff paper for this if used.**

Sample Sentence Sheet to use or copy.

*** This is for the sentences you use in the game for a record and review exercise later.

Sam: You are right. But it is still hard for me. I am so busy.

_____:_____

_____:_____

___:_____

_____:_____

___:_____

_____:_____

___:_____

_____:_____

___:_____

_____:_____

___:_____

_____:_____

_____:_____

_____:_____

___:_____

_____:_____

If you need more paper, add more until you finish the game.

The Game Board

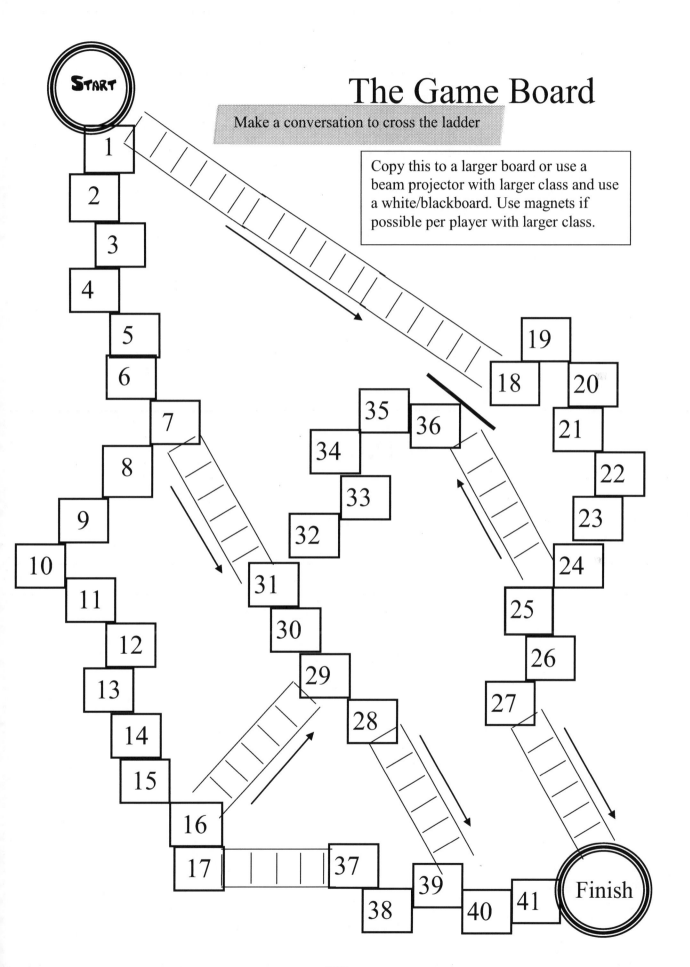

Copy this to a larger board or use a beam projector with larger class and use a white/blackboard. Use magnets if possible per player with larger class.

5 x 5
Plus Bingo

Writing better
to
Communicate

5 by 5 — Writing Plan

- How do you make a move from one idea to another?

- How can you keep a conversation or an essay going?

- The answer is the same for both of these questions.

Transitions!

When you begin a conversation or write an essay you need to make a plan. For a conversation you need to do this in your head.

For an essay, you need to do it on paper.

When you make a plan before you begin you can think better and enjoy the conversation, or writing of an essay better.

The 5x5 Plan

Step 1 — Plan for a topic you can talk about.

- **Talking about a topic that you know about is easier than a new one.** Building vocabulary and knowledge about new topics takes time. Expanding issues may need some research work by the students to make it effective.

Step 2 — List 5 things about the topic

Example — Cars
1. brand
2. speed
3. color
4. price
5. size

Step 3 — Think of 5 good questions for *each idea.*

Example — Cars — **brand**

Which is the best **brand** of car?

What do I like about my **brand**?

Why do I like my **brand**?

How did I choose my **brand**?

When is the best time to buy my **brand**?

Step 4 — Write an answer to the five questions in a complete sentence.

Example —

Q1. **Which** *is the best brand* of car?

Answer - I think that —
        In my opinion **BMW** *is the best brand.*

What is a good NEXT question which is **natural** in your thinking?

2. _____?

Answer — Because _____

3. _____?

Answer _____.

4. _____?

Answer _____.

5. _____?

Answer _____.

Continue with this until **all** the **5 topics + 5 questions** have **5 answers.**

Step 5 — Write an introduction to the topic.

This helps you organise your mind. **When your mind is organised it is easier to have a conversation.**

■ You will listen better and you will enjoy the conversation better.

✦ To help you increase your listening focus, try some lessons in line dancing. This will help you focus on listening and acting together.

℘ ℘ ℘ **Notes** ℘ ℘ ℘

✦ Some students will need more time to process this idea. Other students will grasp it without any problem.

Low – Students at the lower level should be encouraged to develop the idea in groups. Make this a project versus a personal essay.

Intermediate — At this level the student may experience some problems with creating good questions for the five different topics. If you have a beam projector use a computer to help the students. Have them put their ideas on the screen, using the computer. Then offer some corrections to work with. Save it as a file and have the students use it to help them develop their idea.

High — High level students should have no problem developing this idea. Encourage them to develop the idea farther or longer should be the focus for the teacher.

✦ The following segment will **take the student through examples** of a **conversation development**, from start to finish. The student will be shown **how to develop ideas simply** for either conversation, or **simple essay writing**. You have learned about introductions in conversations. Now it is time to develop a conversation. The student will also learn to make a simple introduction for an essay and write a 5 paragraph essay plus an introduction.

℘ ℘ ℘

Let's Try Making an Essay

TOPIC — CARS

✦ An introduction in an essay is **about everything you want to talk about in the essay in one paragraph.**

✦ You have now made a lot of sentences about cars. Let's make an ESSAY introduction to this topic using them.

Example~~

Cars! They are very exciting sometimes and come out with new styles and colours every year. I collect toy cars and make them with my Lego blocks. I like the BMW the best. It is a world famous brand and very fast.

☙ ☙ ☙ Notes ☙ ☙ ☙

What's next?
    It will be a transition to the next paragraph.

Which transitions make sense?

~~ Transitions can be a word or a sentence.
~~ Transitions can change the direction of a conversation.

✦ Comparison transitions <u>help me think of</u> **two or more choices**.

✦ A question transition <u>helps me focus</u> on a **new topic or direction**.

What transitions did we use in the conversation about cars?

Is this different than a conversation?

A good ESSAY will interact with the listener, and a good conversation needs to interact with a listener.

☙ ☙ ☙

~~ More About Transitions

What are some that we use a lot in our writing and speaking for comparisons?

✦ **But** = positive ⟶ negative
However = *more to think about*
Therefore = *to finish the idea*

Some others that show time are ~~

Then = *After A then B*
Whenever = *at anytime* + first action

Here are some others that show time ~ *Memorize them*

After   before   currently   during   eventually finally

first, second... etc.   formerly   immediately   initially   lastly

later   meanwhile   next   previously   simultaneously   soon

Using the Transitions

Example ~~

I collect toy cars and used to make cars with Lego. I don't have money for many real cars.

What's next?

Use transitions from the list to finish this conversation **about cars**.

Or

Change the topic **to one you like by using transition words or questions**.

Or

Finish the Essay **that you started on the previous pages**.

Let's Play Mini Bingo

Step 1 – Make Bingo Cards (Low Level Basic)

You can do this by making a copy of the cards below. Write the transition words (From the list given) and the small words from the previous list found in the Small Words chapter.

B	I	N	G	O
After			Next	
				since
		Before		
Formerly				
but				soon

Choose the number of words you want to work with. If you have many students use them all. Make enough copies of this box so that students have a choice. 25 words will make a maximum of 5 different sheets.

The "caller" for the words will say, "Under the B but ~~ Under the O since". The first person to have 5 in a row can win. There are many different kinds of rows and rules to decide what makes a BINGO before you play.

Step 2 ~~ Intermediate Level

Choose the number of words you want to work with. If you have many students use them all. Make enough copies of this box so that students have a choice. 25 words will make a maximum of 5 different sheets.

Change --- Have a student begin by choosing a word on their BINGO sheet. This will replace the Caller.

Ask another student to use the word in a sentence correctly. If the student uses it correctly you mark the word used on your paper.

Write the sentence on the board.

Step 3 ~~ Advanced Level

The same as Level 2 with one more idea.

Copy the sentences from the board. Challenge the students to make the best story they can from the copied sentences. The best story gets a prize determined by the teacher. Use teams in class or a personal essay for homework.

Play for money

Have everyone put a coin of not more than a quarter or 100 Won in a cup.

The first person to get a **BLACK OUT BINGO** gets half of the money.

The best story with all the sentences wins the other half.

Make your own cards which are bigger for a bigger challenge.

Have Fun

5 x 5
Expanded

Outlining your idea
For
Writing or Conversation

Outlining

~~ **M**aking an outline **helps writing become faster.**

~~ **M**aking an outline makes **finding problems faster and easier.**

~~ **M**aking an outline helps us **think better in a conversation.**

∞ ∞ ∞ **Notes** ∞ ∞ ∞

The bigger the outline *the* **faster**, **easier**, *and* **better** *the* **conversation or essay**,

- Use simple sentences to make an outline about a topic you want to talk about.

- Use the four (4) key ideas you have learned (time, action, motion, emotion) + small words and transitions.

- **The following example will help the student focus on the process.**

- Make full sentences for the answers to give you the paragraph later. You will have one (1) Major topic and five (5) ideas with 25 sentences (5 X 5).

- Use them to create one expanded outline —- a one page essay on one topic — a conversation with another person.

∞ ∞ ∞

Let's try 5x5 Together

Choose your Topic _____

I. Idea (ONE WORD)_____
    A. About the topic — **focus on or about the one word** — use Time or transition to start is good. _____
    B. _____
    C. _____
    D. _____
    E. _____

II. Idea (ONE WORD) _____
    A. About the topic — **focus on or about the one word** — use Time or transition to start is good. _____
    B. _____
    C. _____
    D. _____
    E. _____

III. Idea (ONE WORD) _____
    A. About the topic — **focus on or about the one word** — use Time or transition to start is good. _____
    B. _____
    C. _____
    D. _____
    E. _____

IV. Idea (ONE WORD) _____
    A. About the topic — **focus on or about the one word** — use Time or transition to start is good. _____
    B. _____
    C. _____
    D. _____
    E. _____

V. Idea (ONE WORD) _____
    A. About the topic — **focus on or about the one word** — use Time or transition to start is good. _____
    B. _____
    C. _____
    D. _____
    E. _____

This outline follows the one we did before with cars. The difference is that this is an essay not conversation. The 5 ideas + 5 questions and answers will give you a good outline to start. Just add the introduction and conclusion.

ᘇ ᘇ ᘇ

The Essay

An essay has three parts Introduction — Body — Conclusion

Introduction

The Introduction is everything you want to write about the topic.
5– 8 sentences

The example of cars is used to help you.

Body

The Body is the collection of all your sentences.
under the topics 1,2,3,4,5

5– 8 sentences

Conclusion

The Conclusion is your opinion of what you wrote.
5– 8 sentences

The Conversation

A conversation works best in a question/answer format.

Find a partner or two and make a conversation using the sentences you have made.

You will have to CHANGE or ADD questions to make this work.

Put in the small words and transitions to help make this conversation.

Change topics at least once per person.

On the next two or three pages I have made some lines to write on for practice.

Sam: _____

_____ : _____

_____ : _____

_____ : _____

_____ : _____

_____ : _____

_____ : _____

_____ : _____

_____ : _____

_____ : _____

Final Activities

Final Thoughts
for
A brighter future

Thinking

What topics do I like to talk about?

CHOOSING TOPICS YOU LIKE TO CHAT ABOUT MAKES IT EASIER TO BEGIN AND CONTROL A CONVERSATION.

What topic would you like to talk about?

CHOOSE ONE OR TWO TOPICS TO EXPAND ON. TRYING TO TALK ABOUT TOO MANY THINGS IS CONFUSING AND FRUSTRATING.

IF YOU GET CONFUSED REMEMBER IT IS THE QUESTIONS THAT HELP YOU.

ASK A LOT OF QUESTIONS TO HELP YOU GET BACK TO THE TOPIC YOU WANT TO TALK ABOUT.

Why do I want to talk about it?

DO YOU WANT INFORMATION?

DO YOU WANT TO DEVELOP A COMMON INTEREST?

YOU ARE INTERESTED AND CURIOS SO TALKING ABOUT IT WITH PEOPLE WILL HELP YOU EXPAND YOUR VOCABULARY AND UNDERSTANDING.

When is a good time to talk about it?
One-one, group, quiet, noisy, night club, over coffee, etc.

CHOOSING THE BEST PLACE TO TALK WILL HELP YOU UNDERSTAND BETTER AT THE LEVEL YOU ARE AT. THE LOUDER PLACES ARE HARD TO HEAR AND CONVERSATION IS MUCH HARDER. CHOOSE A GOOD TIME TOO. CHOOSE A TIME WHEN YOU HAVE MORE ENERGY BECAUSE IT IS EASIER TO LISTEN AND FOCUS WHEN YOU HAVE ENERGY.

Final Activity

Who would you like to talk with about this topic?
Anybody, teacher, close friend, etc.

CHOOSING THE RIGHT PERSON GIVES YOU THE BEST CONVERSATION, YOU CHOOSE A TOPIC FOR THE PERSON YOU WANT TO TALK WITH, THIS MAKES TALKING EASIER AND MORE COMFORTABLE,

Can I change the topic so I am more comfortable?

PREPARE AND LEARN TRANSITIONS SO YOU CAN CHANGE THE TOPIC IF YOU ARE ASKED A QUESTION YOU DO NOT LIKE,

How do I stop the conversation or exit it?

STOPPING A CONVERSATION IS NOT SO HARD, ALL YOU HAVE TO DO IS NOT ASK A QUESTION, IF YOU JUST SAY YES AND NO AND THE CONVERSATION WILL STOP NATURALLY,

As a final Activity we will start with one person.

THE FIRST PERSON WILL CHOOSE A TOPIC TO START.

This first person will choose another student to have a conversation with.

This conversation will continue with five questions or ideas from the topic.

Then the second person will choose a third person and continue or change the topic using a transition.

The first person can sit down and watch.

This will continue until all the students have had a chance.

I hope you have had Fun.

Questionnaire.

These are questions that help me the Author make this better. Please fill them out and email your answers and comments to me.

Presentation
— Did you enjoy the Book?   Yes   no
— Did the style help you or hinder your enjoyment? Help   Hinder

Topics
— Were the topics systematic for good understanding?   Yes   No
— Was there a good flow from one section to another?

Was the Book something you would recommend to another teacher? Yes No

Would you like to come to a Seminar to study the book?

5.   Would you like to teach this book to your class?

What did you like most about this book?

_____

_____

_____

What would you change in this book?

_____

_____

_____

email dreams_wb@email.com

You can also photocopy a page if you want to recommend a friend to look at it.

ESL

E is for easy
The desire of the student heart.
E is for energy
Without I cannot do without.
E is for English
Making my stomach squeamish
E is for everything
I dream about.
S is for salty.
From the sweat of study
S is for study.
Seemingly endless
S is for security
Which is my hope.
S is for stupid teachers
Or maybe me.
L is for long and boring
Classes forever.
L is for leisure
A life of pleasure.
L is for love
Which no one can shove.

ESL

Paul Friesen